New Action Sports

Skateboarding Basics

by Jackson Jay

C A P S T O N E   P R E S S

M A N K A T O

C A P S T O N E   P R E S S
818 North Willow Street • Mankato, MN 56001

Printed in the United States of America.

Jay, Jackson.
 Skateboarding basics / Jackson Jay.
 p. cm.
 Includes bibliographical references and index.
 Summary: Describes the history, equipment, and techniques involved in the sport of skateboarding.
 ISBN: 1-56065-374-4
 1. Skateboarding--Juvenile literature. [1. Skateboarding.]
I. Title
 GV859.8.J39   1996
 796.21--dc20   95-44719
                                          CIP
                                          AC

Photo credits

Visuals Unlimited/W.S. Ormerod, Jr.: pp. 4, 12, 32.
Allsport: pp. 7, 18, 21
Charles W. Melton: pp. 8, 11, 15, 16, 23, 24, 27, 29, 30, 34, 37, 41, 42.

Table of Contents

Words in **boldface** type in the text are defined
in the Glossary in the back of this book.

Chapter 1

The World of Skateboarding

To see the world the way a skateboarder does, think of a city street. Imagine the sidewalk and a curb. Think of a bench near a bus stop. Imagine steps and a handrail.

It is just a regular city street to most people. But it is not regular to a skateboarder.

To someone on a skateboard the street is a playground. Skateboarders see a thousand possibilities. They imagine speeding down the sidewalk. They see themselves jumping over a

Skateboarders know the freedom of flying through the air.

fire hydrant. They want to fly over the steps and slide down the handrail.

The **urban landscape** is the skateboarder's paradise. If you decide to become a skateboarder, you will see the world in a new way, too. Regular objects will become challenges. Things and places you never noticed will suddenly stand out.

Flying Through the Air

As a skateboarder, you will feel like you have been given a new pair of eyes. You will discover the speed of racing. You will find the freedom of flying through the air.

When you get good enough, you will learn tricks. Before you know it, you will be skating along with other skateboarders you have met on the streets. You will try to do better tricks than your friends. Then they will try to do better tricks than you.

In skateboarder **lingo,** you will be **thrashin'.**

Skateboards have been around nearly as long as roller skates.

6

Chapter 2

When Skateboarding Began

Skateboards have been around as long as roller skates. Nearly 100 years ago, young people nailed roller skates to boards and rode them. Sometimes they sat on the boards. Sometimes they stood up.

Factory-made skateboards appeared in the 1960s. At the time, young people were crazy about surfing. People were watching surfing movies. They were singing surfing songs. They were wearing surfing clothes. Surfing was a big **fad**.

Skateboarding evolved from surfing.

A group of surfers at the Val Surf shop in California built and sold skateboards. They wanted people to be able to surf on dry land. Skateboarding was called sidewalk surfing. People who never got near a surfboard or an ocean learned to be great sidewalk surfers.

Early skateboards were not as good as today's boards.

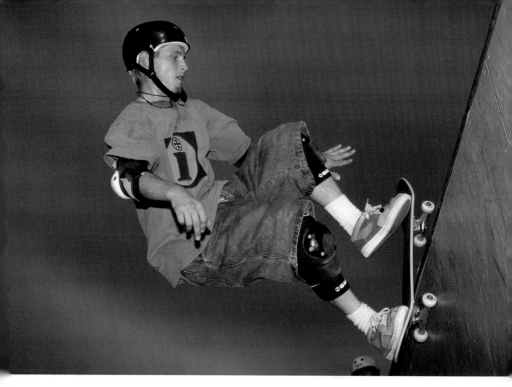

Toward the end of the '60s, skateboarding died out.

Early Boards

Early skateboards were different from boards today. They were flat, short, and stiff. The wheels were like roller-skate wheels. They were made of clay and were very hard.

The skater could not make tight turns. The wheels would stop turning when they hit a pebble or a crack in the sidewalk. Still, skateboarding was new and exciting. More than a million skateboards were sold.

Skating styles were pretty simple. Most skaters rushed down hills or weaved back and forth.

The Fad Dies

Toward the end of the 1960s, both the surfing and skateboarding fads ended. Some people think skateboarding died out because it was unsafe.

Drivers were worried about skaters getting hit by cars. People on the sidewalks worried about getting hit by skaters. Some parents would not let their kids ride skateboards. Some towns even passed laws against skateboarding. For almost 10 years, there was very little skating going on.

But there were still some **diehard rippers** who never quit. They kept the sport alive. They even invented new ways to ride. So when skateboarding became popular again, it was more exciting than ever.

Urethane wheels made skateboarding popular again.

The New Boom in Boarding

In the 1970s, roller skates were made with **urethane** wheels. Urethane wheels were softer than clay wheels. They gripped the road better. They rolled over cracks and pebbles easily. A surfer named Frank Nasworthy thought the new wheels would be great for skateboards.

His idea started a new life for skateboarding. Skaters tried more tricks because they had better wheels. They began to jump up on park benches. They rode around inside empty swimming pools. They jumped over fire hydrants and parked cars. They pushed the limits of riding.

This new breed of skaters wanted better equipment. So skateboard makers stopped using roller-skate parts. Parts were made just for skateboards.

Skateboards are still pretty simple.

Chapter 3
Gearing Up Safely

Skateboards are still pretty simple. There is a board to stand on. There are wheels to roll on. Parts called **trucks** steer the skateboards.

But there are differences. There are stiff boards and soft boards. There are fast wheels and slow wheels. There are different ways of adjusting the trucks for a harder or softer ride. You can make the best choice when you buy a board if you know these differences.

The board is also called a deck.

The nose and tail of this board curve upward.

Boards

The board is also called a deck. Fiberglass
and aluminum are sometimes used to make
boards. Most skaters, however, think that
maple **plywood** makes the best boards.

18

In the last few years, boards have gotten lighter and narrower. Today the average skateboard has a deck about 30 inches (76 centimeters) long and eight inches (20 centimeters) wide. But that is just the basic shape. There are many differences among individual boards.

One difference is the wheelbase. Wheelbase is the distance between the trucks. On a shorter board, the trucks will be closer together. A short wheelbase means a board can make tighter turns. But it is less stable than a board with a longer wheelbase.

Another difference is in the **flex** of the board. A low-flex or soft board is good for doing tricks. It is not as stable, though. A high-flex board, on the other hand, might have too much spring. It can throw a rider off.

A board's nose and tail usually curve up. The nose is the part of the board that hangs over the front truck. The tail is the part of the board that hangs over the back truck.

Curved noses and tails give a skater's back foot something to press against. That makes it easier to do tricks. Most street skaters like six to seven inches (15 to 18 centimeters) for a tail and five and one-half to six and one-half inches (14 to 17 centimeters) for a nose.

Stiff boards with wheels and trucks for all-purpose street riding are good for beginners. A stiff board is harder to turn, but it is more stable. Beginners will not get thrown off as much while they learn to ride.

Some experienced skaters buy the trucks, wheels, and board separately. Then they put together their own skateboards. They even buy unpainted boards. Then they put their own colors and designs on them.

Wheels

Skateboard wheels are made of urethane. They can be made with different degrees of

Most skateboards are made of maple plywood.

hardness. Softer wheels are better for fast turns back and forth. Harder wheels are better for building up speed.

Wheels are measured in millimeters. For many years, skaters liked wheels that were 55 to 66 millimeters tall and 50 to 60 millimeters wide. But the wheels have been getting smaller, just like the boards. Now 45 or 46 millimeters is common. Smaller wheels let skaters turn quickly. These wheels do not go as fast, but they are easier to use for tricks.

A lot of ramp skaters still like the larger wheels. They are faster and easier to control.

Trucks

The real work of a skateboard is done by the trucks. Trucks work as **axles** between the wheels. They also steer the board. If you fly into the air, they serve as landing gear. The trucks take a lot of punishment. They have to be made well.

Grip tape keeps a boarder's feet from slipping off the board.

The most popular trucks are made of heat-treated aluminum. They have steel axles and steel kingpins. The kingpin is the post that connects the axle to the baseplate. The

Larger wheels are faster and easier to control.

baseplate is the part that attaches to the bottom of the board.

When you stand on a skateboard and lean to one side, the trucks pivot on the kingpin. They pivot in the direction you are leaning. If you lean to the right, the board turns to the right. If you lean to the left, the board turns to the left.

Trucks can be adjusted to fit the way you ride. If you tighten the nut on the kingpin, your turns will be stiffer. The board will not be so wobbly when it goes fast. If you loosen the nut, the trucks will pivot more easily. The board will turn quickly, but it will be wobbly.

It is good to know how to adjust a board. You might find one you like that is too wobbly for you. Before you give up on the board, see if adjusting the trucks will fix the problem.

The Extras

Grip tape is the main extra feature added to a skateboard. Grip tape is a material like sandpaper that keeps your feet from slipping off the board. A lot of boards come with grip tape on them. If yours does not, you can buy some and put it on yourself.

Some people add plastic rails to the bottom of their boards. These help the board slide along curbs and benches. They also prevent damage to the board. Noseguards and tailguards are available, too.

These items add weight to your board. The screws needed to mount them can weaken the plywood. Think carefully before you add extras.

Some rails have stick-on backs. Then you do not need screws.

Maintenance

Make sure you check your gear before you ride. You can catch little problems before they become big ones. Keeping your board in top shape means it will last longer and perform better.

Wheels usually wear out first. You can make your wheels last longer by rotating them as

Knee pads, elbow pads, and a helmet will protect skaters trying dangerous moves.

they wear down. To do this, take the wheels off the axles. Turn them around. Then put them back on. This will make them wear evenly.

Always check the nuts and bolts on your trucks. If you can turn any of them with your fingers, they are too loose. They should be tightened. Check the adjustment on your kingpin. Set it the way you like it.

Part of the truck is the bushing. This is the plastic piece on the kingpin. It acts as a shock absorber. If it is worn out or poorly made, it can make your ride terrible. Check the bushing and replace it if needed.

Check your skate deck, too. Even a good maple plywood board can wear out. Sometimes the glue does not hold the wood together. The layers start to separate.

This skater keeps one hand on the board for control.

Keep knees bent and flexible while on the half-pipe.

A crack can be stopped with a little glue and a wood clamp. Squirt the glue into the crack. Spread it thin. Put on the clamp. Leave the board overnight. When it is completely dry, sand the edges of the board until they are smooth.

Safety Equipment

It is easy to hurt yourself while skateboarding. It is smart to protect yourself.

The basic safety gear includes a helmet, wrist guards, kneepads, and elbow pads. Get good ones. They will last longer and keep you safe.

Some skaters wear gloves to protect against scrapes and cuts. You can even glue plastic on the palms and fingers of your gloves. The plastic adds protection and makes the gloves last longer.

Many skaters wear high-top sneakers for ankle support. There are also shoes with extra padding made just for skaters. They have strips of leather or plastic on areas that get a lot of wear.

Chapter 4

The Basics of Boarding

After you pick out a board, you should find out if you have a regular **stance** or a **goofy-foot** stance. To do this, stand with your feet across the board while you hold on to someone. First, stand with your right foot in front. Then turn around and stand with your left foot in front.

If you are more comfortable with your left foot in front, you have a regular stance. If you are more comfortable with your right foot in front, you have a goofy-foot stance.

Skaters have either a regular stance or a goofy-foot stance.

While you are on the board, bend your knees slightly. Try shifting your weight forward to your toes. Then shift back toward your heels.

Feel how the board wobbles from side to side. Shift your weight from one foot to the

Tricks are a fun part of skating.

other. Feel how the board tips to the front and to the back. With enough practice, your board will feel like part of your body. Take all the time you need to get the board under control.

Practice Riding

Find a parking lot or a playground away from traffic to practice. Try gliding. To do this, place your front foot in the middle of the board. Point it forward. Use your back foot to push off and glide. Do not put your back foot on yet. Just glide a bit.

The board will probably kick out away from you a few times. You might even fall. Do not let that stop you. Keep practicing. Soon you will get the hang of it.

When you feel good about gliding, try placing your back foot on the board. Put the back foot across the width of the board. Then turn your front foot so it is also across the board. Bend your knees a little and keep a wide, comfortable stance.

It will not be long before you find where your feet work best. Repeat this until you can step on the board easily and take a solid stance.

Turning

Now try turning. With your knees bent, shift your weight to your toes and see how the board turns. That is called a **frontside** turn. If you lean back on your heels, the board will go into a **backside** turn.

Frontside and backside turns are the keys to controlling a skateboard. Do one and then the other as you travel forward. Draw the letter S with your board. Keep your arms and upper body loose. Find your balance and learn to use just the right amount of pressure.

Hitting the Streets

When you think you are ready, look for a short and easy hill. Find one away from traffic. You only need 30 or 40 feet (nine or 12 meters) of gentle slope. Aim your board downhill. Plant your front foot. Push off and skate.

The action can be awesome at skating parks.

When you first start out, it is easy to lose control of a skateboard. Do not be afraid to jump off the board.

To jump as you are riding down a hill, lift your back foot. Then step forward off the board. Run a few steps until you can stop safely.

The weight of your front foot will kick the board up the hill behind you. You will be able to catch it when it comes down.

If you jump off at a faster speed, you will simply run more steps. You might even go so fast that you will fall. You need to learn how to fall right, too.

Falling Safely

When you fall, it might be natural to hold your arms out. Your instinct tells you to try to catch yourself with your hands. Do not do it. You could break your wrists.

The best way to fall is to hold your elbows in and roll. Roll on your shoulder. Practice a few falls on the grass. After a few times, you will be able to jump up after almost any crash.

Make sure you take plenty of time learning how to ride, how to turn, and how to jump off. If you do the basics well, you will pick up tricks faster. You will be safer, too.

Tricks

Tricks are a big part of skating. You will probably want to learn some. Almost every

Many towns have special skate parks.

skater learns how to do **wheelies** and **ollies.** As you skate more, you will meet other skaters who will help you.

Every new trick builds on the one that came before it. Take your time. Do not try a new move until you are ready. If you are patient, you will get the hang of it.

Parks and Streets

Even though skateboarding is a popular sport, some areas do not allow it. A lot of skateboarders find that city officials frown on the sport. Some cities do not allow skateboarding on public streets.

They are right to be concerned. You can get hurt if you collide with a bicycle, motorcycle, car, or truck.

Now there are special skate parks. They have skateboarding areas with bumps and

If you can do the basics well, you will learn tricks faster.

ramps. Some even have empty swimming pools for boarding.

The action at skate parks can be awesome. Skaters fly up and over ramps. They spin around and land backwards. Some do handstands at the top of an empty pool. Others hold the board with one hand, then go roaring down to the bottom.

Play it Safe

Your job as a skateboarder is to play it safe. That includes using safety gear and obeying the laws. If you do not know what the laws are, call or visit your local police station. You can also get information from a local skateboard shop.

All skateboarders want to get thrashin'. But do not push your limits until you feel ready. Experienced skaters who do the wildest tricks have practiced for a long time.

One day it will all come together. Trust yourself. You will know when you are ready. Then, and only then, let it rip.

It is important to wear safety gear when thrashin'.

Glossary

axle—a rod that connects two wheels

backside—the side of the skateboard where the skater places the heels

diehard rippers—dedicated skateboarders

fad—popular activity people are interested in for a short time

flex—the ability of a board to bend

frontside—the side of the skateboard where the skater places the toes

goofy foot—standing with your right foot forward on a board

lingo—special words and a special way of talking used by groups who share an activity

ollie—jumping in the air with a skateboard

plywood—thick wood made by gluing many thin pieces together

stance—the way you stand on a skateboard

thrashin'—performing exciting tricks

trucks—the hardware on a skateboard that includes axles, kingpin, and bushings

urban landscape—streets, buildings, parking lots, and other objects that make up a city

urethane—a special, strong chemical compound

wheelies—riding the board with the front wheels off the ground

To Learn More

Evans, Jeremy. *Skateboarding.* New York: Crestwood House, 1994.

Gutman, Bill. *Skateboarding.* New York: Tor Books, 1995.

Shoemaker, Joel. *Skateboarding Streetstyle.* Minneapolis: Capstone Press, 1995.

Wilkins, Kevin. *Skateboarding.* Philadelphia: Running Press, 1994.

You can read articles about skateboarding in *Slap* magazine.

Useful Addresses

National Recreation and Park Association
2775 South Quincy Avenue
Suite 300
Arlington, VA 22206-2204

United Skateboard Federation
P.O. Box 30004
San Bernardino, CA 92413

Woodward Training Center
Box 93, Route 45
Woodward, PA 16882

Visalia YMCA Skate Camp
211 West Tulare Avenue
Visalia, CA 93277

Index